artworld

What Is

MODERNISM?

by Kate Riggs

CREATIVE EDUCATION • CREATIVE PAPERBACKS

Published by Creative Education and Creative Paperbacks
P.O. Box 227, Mankato, Minnesota 56002
Creative Education and Creative Paperbacks are
imprints of The Creative Company
www.thecreativecompany.us

Design and production by Chelsey Luther·
Art direction by Rita Marshall
Printed in the United States of America

Photographs by Alamy (Willem de Kooning/Peter van Evert, flab,
Nam June Paik/B Christopher, Tracey Whitefoot), Art Resource (Roy
Lichtenstein/Smithsonian American Art Museum, Washington, DC;
National Portrait Gallery, Smithsonian Institution; Jackson Pollock/
Centre Pompidou; Mark Rothko), Corbis (Corbis, FONDAZIONE/ANSA),
Flickr (Tanaka Atsuko/Thomas Stellmach, Claes Oldenburg & Coosje
van Bruggen/Danny Birchall), Getty Images (Tanaka Atsuko/Lucas
Schifres/Stringer), Wikimedia Creative Commons (Piet Mondriaan/
Gemeentemuseum Den Haag)

Library of Congress Cataloging-in-Publication Data
Riggs, Kate.
What is modernism? / Kate Riggs.
p. cm. — (Art world)
Summary: With prompting questions and historical background, an
early reader comes face to face with famous works of Modern art and is
encouraged to identify images and consider different meanings.
Includes bibliographical references and index.
ISBN 978-1-60818-627-3 (hardcover)
ISBN 978-1-62832-225-5 (pbk)
ISBN 978-1-56660-693-6 (eBook)
1. Modernism (Art)—Juvenile literature. I. Title.

N6494.M64R54 2016
709.04—dc23   2015008502

CCSS: RI.1.1, 2, 3, 5, 6, 7; RI.2.1, 2, 3, 5, 6, 7; RI.3.1, 3, 5, 7; RF.1.1; RF.2.3, 4;
RF.3.3

First Edition HC
9 8 7 6 5 4 3 2 1
First Edition PBK
9 8 7 6 5 4 3 2 1

Contents

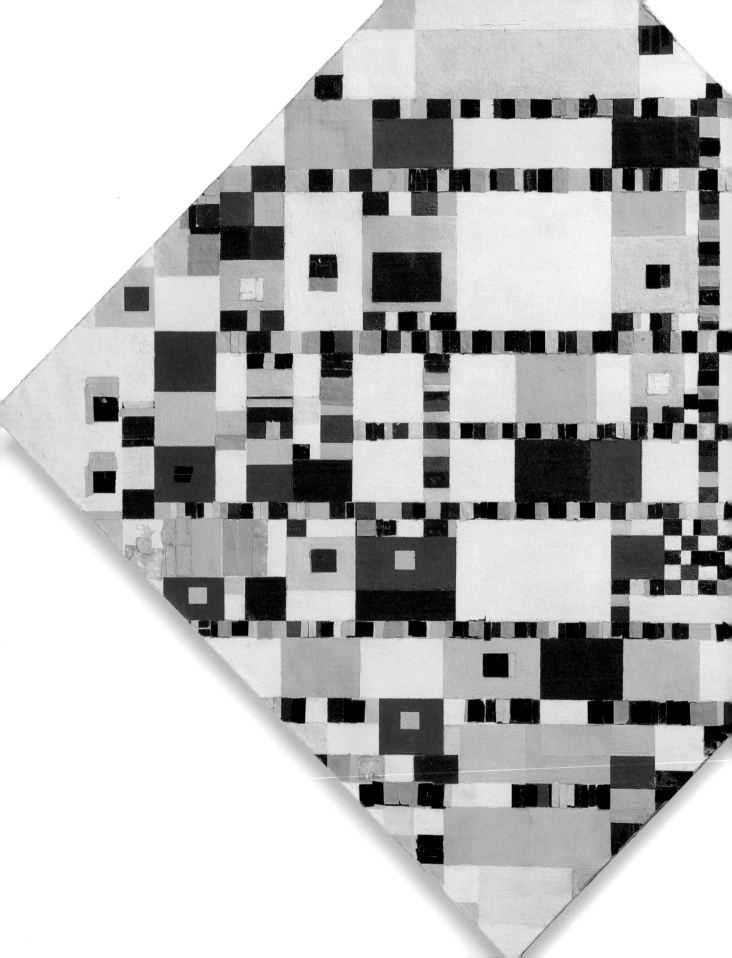

Familiar Forms

Cans of soup are in a row. Blocks of color are stacked together. Are you in a store or looking at a canvas? If you see everyday things, you may be looking at Modern art.

Dutch artist Piet Mondrian helped start Modern art.

Becoming Modern

The world changed a lot in the early 1900s.
Modern artists wanted to try new things.
They used colors to show emotions. Their
pictures did not look like real life!

Left: *Black Spot* (1912), by Wassily Kandinsky;
above: *Composition* (1955), by Willem de Kooning

Colors on Colors

Later, Mark Rothko painted simple shapes and colors. His *No. 12* (1954) is huge! It swallows you in color!

Rothko called many of his paintings by a number or their colors.

All in Line

Jackson Pollock laid his canvases on the floor. Then he poured or splashed the paint on top. Try to follow the lines in his *Number 26 A, Black and White* (1948). Do they make you sway?

Left: Pollock at work; above: *Number 26 A*

Parade of Flags

Jasper Johns painted more familiar images and numbers. After *Flag* (1954), Johns painted many American flags. Each was different. What do you think of when you look at a flag?

Johns said that a dream made him start painting *Flag*.

How many cans do you see in this close-up?

Mm, Good!

Looking at a can of soup may make you hungry. What if you saw hundreds? Andy Warhol's *200 Campbell's Soup Cans* (1962) all look the same at first. But some have different names. Others have different colors.

Automated Art

Today, computers and videos can make and be part of Modern art. Robots can even paint pictures! There are as many kinds of Modern art as people can dream up.

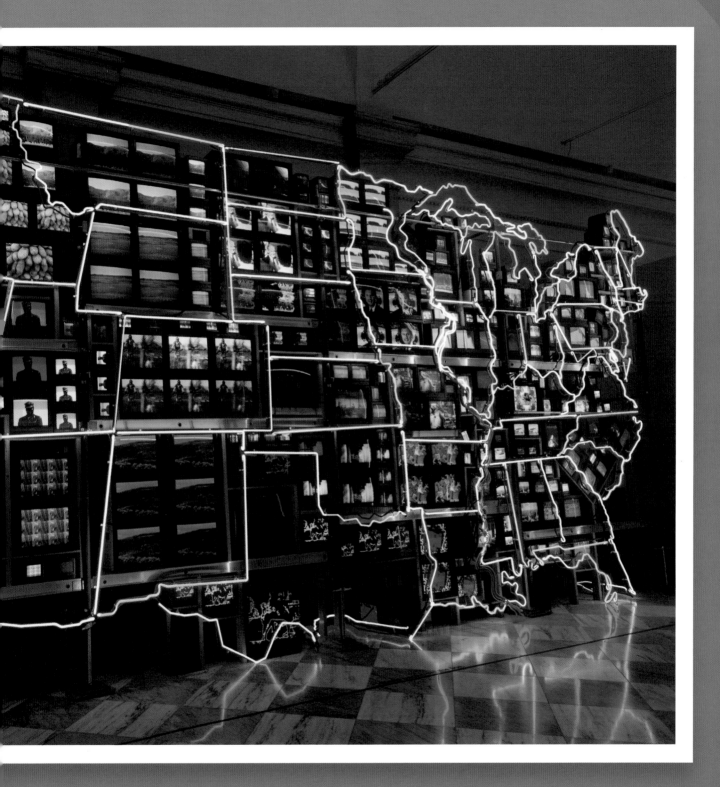

Electronic Superhighway: Continental U.S. (1995), by Nam June Paik

Above: *Reverie* (1965), by Roy Lichtenstein; right: *Big Sweep* (2006), by Claes Oldenburg and Coosje van Bruggen

Modern Art and You

What kinds of lines do you see in a Modern art piece? Are there any pictures you recognize? Think about what those pictures mean to you!

Portrait of a Modern Artist

Atsuko Tanaka was born in Japan. She made a
kind of Modern art called performance art. In 1956,
she made a dress made of colored light bulbs and
wires. The dress plugged in. Atsuko's face showed
at the top of the glowing lights.

Left: *Electric Dress* (1956); above: *93C*

Glossary

canvas—a piece of strong cloth on which people can paint

emotions—feelings such as happiness, sadness, fearfulness, and excitement

performance art—a form of art that a person does or acts out

Read More

Friedman, Samantha. *Matisse's Garden*. New York: Museum of Modern Art, 2014.

Rubin, Susan Goldman. *Andy Warhol: Pop Art Painter*. New York: Abrams, 2007.

Websites

ArtThink: Detail Detective
http://www.sfmoma.org/artthink/toolsandgames.asp
Look carefully at these pictures from Modern artists to train your artistic eye!

Art Projects for Kids
http://artprojectsforkids.org/portfolio/16909/
Create your own soup flavors and make a set of soup-can art inspired by Andy Warhol.

NOTE: Every effort has been made to ensure that the websites listed above are suitable for children, that they have educational value, and that they contain no inappropriate material. However, because of the nature of the Internet, it is impossible to guarantee that these sites will remain active indefinitely or that their contents will not be altered.

Index